WALKING

In The

FOOTSTEPS

Of

GOD

<u>Daily Devotional</u>

GEORGE A. COPELAND

Serenity Publishing & Communications, Inc.
www.serenitypc.com

ISBN: 0-9763698-9-3

Dedication

To Evangelist Susie M. Copeland
Thank you for your love and support of my
ministry through the years.

And to my children, Marsha, Mandell, Yolanda,
Joshua, and Christina

And my eight wonderful grandchildren, Desiree,
George M. Jr., Darian, Dustin, Jeremiah, Daijah,
Trinity, and Madison

I would also like to say a special thanks to:
Bishop Charles E. Williams
Dr. Kevin Williams
Apostle Lobias Murray
Apostle Richard Taylor
Evangelist Steve Mc Queen
Elder Thomas Hoy
Prophet Brian Mosley
The United Faith Churches of Deliverance family

Also special thanks to the following for their help
on this project:
Dean Annie Brookes
Sis. Stephanie Pope
Sis. Tanya Justice
Sherrie Cole
Carlton Holbrook
Jackie Hayward
Linwood Corbin

Introduction

There are many who say that it is impossible to have a relationship with God. So the premise of the title of this book will challenge many, because they perceive God as an 'it' instead of a Him. Yes, He has a personality, feelings and characteristics that can be seen, felt, experienced and appreciated.

Yes, He is the Almighty God, full of grace and power but He is also the God that desires a relationship with you and I. He made that abundantly clear when we see the lengths He went to in order to make sure that a relationship with Him could be had by all who would desire it.

There is a Bible full of promises and thoughts that make this kind of book so useful and rich with pos- sibility. Because as you walk through each day with God, you are bound to become closer and closer to Him. There is no getting around it!

The reality is that as you move into this wonderful relationship, you are also entering a magnificient time to experience the manifestation of the promises of God in your life!

His words are the footsteps that He has made from heaven to earth. Those tracks are still clear as you journey through the pages of His Word. There is no doubt that the sand is fresh, it is as if He just came by your way. So don't hesitate to walk where He has walked and gleen from the words He has spoken to you.

Vision is important. Solomon, t he wisest and richest man who every lived, said, "Without a vision the people perish." (Proverbs 29:18). One must see in his mind's eye what he wants to be or accomplish in this earth realm, then steps must be taken to reach those goals.

As a study shows, 84% of knowledge is received through the eyegate. That is why visuals are so valuable in obtaining knowledge. The Lord's instruction to the prophet Habakkuk, 'Write the vision and make it plain upon tables, that he may run that reads it." (Habakkuk 2:2)

<u>STEP ONE</u>
What one see in his mind's eye, he must clearly make known the plan, thoughts or goal. Write it down on paper so the very thought or idea will not vanish.

In Habakkuk 2:3, the scripture explains that the vision has a due date when it must be completed, so if your goal or vision is written you have crystalized the vision or dream.

STEP TWO
Begin to say it or speak it. It is important to verbalize your vision. It must come out of your mouth.

Proverbs 18:21 (KJV)
A man's belly shall be satisfied with the fruit of his mouth; and with the increase of his lips shall he be filled.

James 3:10 (KJV)
Out of the same mouth proceedeth blessing and cursing. My brethren, these things ought not so to be.

Mark 11:23 (KJV)
For verily I say unto you, That whosoever shall say unto this mountain, Be thou removed, and be thou cast into the sea; and shall not doubt in his heart, but shall believe that those things which he saith shall come to pass; he shall have whatsoever he saith.

Notice the power of the tongue in Mark 11:14, "Then Jesus said to the tree, "May no one ever eat your fruit again!" And the disciples heard him say it."

STEP THREE

We must obtain it.

"The LORD hath been mindful of us: he will bless us; he will bless the house of Israel; he will bless the house of Aaron. He will bless them that fear the LORD, both small and great. The LORD shall increase you more and more, you and your children. Ye are blessed of the LORD which made heaven and earth. The heaven, even the heavens, are the LORD's: but the earth hath he given to the children of men."

Psalm 115:12-16 (KJV)

The earth is ours to take out of it what we need for our existence and our pleasure.

With that thought in mind, this book was written to assist you in following His footsteps throughout your daily life. There is a prayer entry for each day with thoughts, scriptures and personal entries for you to complete. As you move closer to completion of this 30-day journey you will notice areas for you to complete with your own words. Thus, pushing you closer to the hand-held fellowship and prayer life that He desires with you.

As you daily take this tool and apply it to your life, there is no doubt in my mind that you will be able to say, "I am walking in the footsteps of God!"

Bishop George Copeland

Before you can take a walk you need to make sure you are prepared. In this context you will need to make sure you are in a right-standing relationship with the One whose footsteps you are trying to walk in.

So let's get ready to take this journey....but before you do, you will need to ask yourself one question.

Have I accepted the gift of salvation provided by Jesus Christ on Calvary?

Before we can walk with God we must be joined to Him and the only way we can truly be joined to Him is through the acceptance of His most precious gift to us, which is His Son – Jesus!

The days of setting ourselves aside to walk in fellowship with Him through prayer cannot begin until we have made a decision to accept the gift of salvation. If you have this book and find yourself in a place where you need to renew your relationship with God, then now is the time!

Today is the day
of salvation
for you!

REALIZE YOUR CONDITION. THIS IS TO FULLY
UNDERSTAND THAT YOUR SPIRITUAL
CONDITIION HAS TO CHANGE.

And when he came to himself, he said, How many
hired servants of my father's have bread enough
and to spare, and I perish with hunger!

Luke 15:17 (KJV)

This includes a verbal acknowledgement and ad-
mittance of your sins.

Only acknowledge thine iniquity, that thou hast
transgressed against the LORD thy God, and hast
scattered thy ways to the strangers under
every green tree, and ye have not obeyed my voice,
saith the LORD.

Jeremiah 3:13 (KJV)

YOU MUST REPENT, (WHICH IS BEING SORRY
ENOUGH TO STOP THE ACTIONS THAT YOU
SHOULD NOT BE DOING).

The story of the prodigal's son tells us, after he
wasted all his earthly possessions on the fast lane
of life, he ended up in a hog pen so impoverished
that he was about to eat the hog's food. But he
came to himself. One will never see change in life
or circumstances until he or she comes to themselves and recognizes where he or she is currently.

10

I will arise and go to my father, and will say unto him, Father, I have sinned against heaven, and before thee.

Luke 15:18 (KJV)

Therefore I will judge you, O house of Israel, every one according to his ways, saith the Lord GOD. Repent, and turn yourselves from all your transgressions; so iniquity shall not be your ruin.

Ezekiel 18:39 (KJV)

RECEIVE THE RESTORATION THAT REPENTANCE OFFERS

And he arose, and came to his father. But when he was yet a great way off, his father saw him, and had compassion, and ran, and fell on his neck, and kissed him.

Luke 15:20 (KJV)

Turn, O backsliding children, saith the LORD; for I am married unto you: and I will take you one of a city, and two of a family, and I will bring you to Zion:

Jeremiah 3:14 (KJV)

And they shall teach no more every man his neighbour, and every man his brother, saying, Know the LORD: for they shall all know me, from the least of them unto the greatest of them, saith the LORD: for I will forgive their iniquity, and I will remember their sin no more.

Jeremiah 31:34 (KJV)

The LORD hath appeared of old unto me, saying, Yea, I have loved thee with an everlasting love: therefore with loving-kindness have I drawn thee.

Jeremiah 31:3 (KJV)

For I will restore health unto thee, and I will heal thee of thy wounds, saith the LORD; because they called thee an Outcast, saying, This is Zion, whom no man seeketh after.

Jeremiah 30:17 (KJV)

He restoreth my soul: he leadeth me in the paths of righteousness for his name's sake.

Psalm 23:3 (KJV)

REASSURANCE (GOD'S GUARANTEE)

Now unto him that is able to keep you from falling, and to present you faultless before the presence of his glory with exceeding joy,

Jude 1:24 (KJV)

For the which cause I also suffer these things: nevertheless I am not ashamed: for I know whom I have believed, and am persuaded that he is able to keep that which I have committed unto him against that day.

2 Timothy 1:12 (KJV)

After you have entered into this wonderful new relationship, you will need to be able to communicate with God. And the way you do that is the same as with a human being. You will need to talk to Him and He with you; quite simply you need to know how to pray!

Though prayer is communication with God; you talking to Him and Him talking to you, it is much more than that. Prayer brings honor to God. It's an act of worship, giving of homage to the Lord. Prayer also brings about humility. It brings us into a relationship and causes us to depend upon the Lord. We then realize that we can do nothing without Him.

I am the vine, ye are the branches: He that abideth in me, and I in him, the same bringeth forth much fruit: for without me ye can do nothing.

John 15:5 (KJV)

Prayer causes us to receive the things that we ask of God. In praying one should constantly examine his or her motives to insure that he or she is not selfish, or out of line with God's Word.

On the next page are some prayer principles to keep in your heart as you begin to walk in His footsteps.

13

Prayer and Worship
go hand -in- hand.

Prayer prepares
the soul for worship.

Prayer is not an elective
activity but an essential
practice.

If there is no Prayer, then
there is no Life Flow.

Prayer must be a priority.

Prayer allows a person
to have communion with God.

Day 1
"When I Need Direction"

Everyone of us need direction throughout life. No one is exempt from the uncertainty of making a decision that is best in certain circumstances.

The good news is that God is ready to guide us and help us as we lean on Him for His wisdom, guidance and direction. Today, seek the Lord for guidance in your life and I am sure God will lead you in the perfect path He has designed for you.

His Steps...

Psalm 25:9 (NLT)
He leads the humble in what is right, teaching them his way.

Psalm 48:14 (NLT)
For that is what God is like. He is our God forever and ever, and he will be our guide until we die.

Psalm 55:17 (LB)
"I will pray morning, noon and night, pleading aloud with God and He will answer,"

Psalm 119:133 (NIV)
Direct my footsteps according to your word; let no sin rule over me.

Isaiah 48:17 (NLT)

The LORD, your Redeemer, the Holy One of Israel, says: I am the LORD your God, who teaches you what is good and leads you along the paths you should follow.

Isaiah 58:11 (NLT)

The LORD will guide you continually, watering your life when you are dry and keeping you healthy, too. You will be like a well-watered garden, like an ever-flowing spring.

John 11:9 (NLT)

Jesus replied, "There are twelve hours of daylight every day. As long as it is light, people can walk safely. They can see because they have the light of this world.

My Steps...

Father in the name of Jesus, thank you for your word. For the entrance of your word gives light. I thank you for the light that I see and for the scriptures you have laid out before us to guide us day and night.

You told me that you would teach me the ways that are right and best as I humbly turn to you. You promised if I put you first and acknowledged you that you would direct my path.

Lord I thank you for being my Redeemer, O, Holy One of Israel. I thank you for pushing our enemy back. And when we walk contrary to your Word, thank you for chastisement and bringing me back on course.

Thank you for being a mighty God, an everlasting Father, the Prince of Peace. Thank you for inviting me to come walk with you and feel the nearness of you. Lord, bless me day by day. Bring me into that place that I've never known before.

I will forever praise your name. The glory and honor shall forever be yours is my prayer. In Jesus name; Amen.

When You See It...
(Write Your Vision)

_____

_____

_____

_____

_____

Then You'll Say It...
(Speak the Vision)

_____

_____

_____

_____

_____

And You'll Have it!
(Write an Action Plan)

_____

_____

_____

_____

_____

Day 2
"Obtaining My Blessing Today"

God desires to bless you. That is a fact. But we must believe that it is His desire to bless us.

As you medidate on these scriptures, pray that God will bring a greater revelation of this truth that you might receive the great and wonderful blessings He has in store for you!

His Steps...

Exodus 23:25 (NLT)
You must serve only the LORD your God. If you do, I will bless you with food and water, and I will keep you healthy.

Deuteronomy 28:2 (KJV)
And all these blessings shall come on thee, and overtake thee, if thou shall hearken unto the voice of the LORD thy God

Psalms 115:15-16 (KJV)
Ye are blessed of the LORD which made heaven and earth. The heaven, even the heavens, are the LORD's: but the earth hath he given to the children of men.

Psalm 29:11 (KJV)
The LORD will give strength unto his people; the LORD will bless his people with peace.

Psalm 55:22 (KJV)
Cast thy burden upon the LORD, and he shall sustain thee: he shall never suffer the righteous to be moved.

Psalm 84:11 (NLT)
For the LORD God is our light and protector. He gives us grace and glory. No good thing will the LORD withhold from those who do what is right.

Isaiah 44:3 (NLT)
For I will give you abundant water to quench your thirst and to moisten your parched fields. And I will pour out my Spirit and my blessings on your children.

2 Peter 1:3 (KJV)
According as his divine power hath given unto us all things that pertain unto life and godliness, through the knowledge of him that hath called us to glory and virtue:

My Steps...

Father in the Name of Jesus, I thank you for another day to take time to meditate and feast on your word. Lord, thank you for the scriptures I have meditated upon. They have ministered to my heart making me what you have ordained for me to be.

Lord, right now, bless me in abundance and minister to my spirit. I thank you for what I am learning from your word. I thank you for the closeness my spirit feels toward you right now. Oh, Jesus, I feel your presence, your nearness upon my soul, upon my body and my mind.

I appreciate every good and perfect gift. I thank you for considering me, and I know if I was the only person on the earth that you would have still gone to the cross, and shed your blood to save me. Your goal is to teach me to live pleasing to you, how to forgive others and how to forgive myself.

Continue to bless me with yourself is my earnest prayer, in Jesus name. Amen

When You See It...
(Write Your Vision)

_____

_____

_____

_____

_____

Then You'll Say It...
(Speak the Vision)

_____

_____

_____

_____

_____

And You'll Have it!
(Write an Action Plan)

_____

_____

_____

_____

_____

Day 3

"Communicating with a Friend that is Closer than a Brother"

In life, friends come and friends go. Isn't it nice to know that we have a friend that is forever abiding with us and will never leave no matter how bad things get

His Steps...

Proverb 18:24 [AMP]
The man of many friends [a friend of all the world] will prove himself a bad friend, but there is a friend who sticks closer than a brother.

Luke 5:18-20 [NIV]
Some men came carrying a paralytic on a mat and tried to take him into the house to lay him before Jesus. [19]When they could not find a way to do this because of the crowd, they went up on the roof and lowered him on his mat hrough the tiles into the middle of the crowd, right in front of Jesus. When Jesus saw their faith, he said, "Friend, your sins are forgiven."

Proverb 17:17 [NLT]
A friend is always loyal, and a brother is born to help in time of need.

John 15:13-16 (NIV)

Greater love has no one than this, that he lay down his life for his friends. You are my friends if you do what I command. I no longer call you servants, because a servant does not know his master's business. Instead, I have called you friends, for everything that I learned from my Father I have made known to you. You did not choose me, but I chose you and appointed you to go and bear fruit–fruit that will last. Then the Father will give you whatever you ask in my name.

John 13:34 (NLT)

So now I am giving you a new commandment: Love each other. Just as I have loved you, you should love each other.

Amos 3:3 (NLT)

Can two people walk together without agreeing on the direction?

Proverb 27:17 (NLT)

As iron sharpens iron, a friend sharpens a friend.

My Steps...

Father in the name of Jesus, I thank you for your word, which I depend on. I thank you for being my friend. I trust your word and I know it will not fail me. I thank you Lord, for all you've done in my life.

I thank you for rebuking the enemy for my sake and for putting him under my feet. I am thankful to you for teaching me how to triumph in you, through your word. Lord, bless me throughout this day.

And because I know you are doing these things for me, I will be forever careful to give your name the praise. The glory and honor is yours is my prayer in Jesus' name. Amen.

When You See It...
(Write Your Vision)

_____

_____

_____

_____

_____

Then You'll Say It...
(Speak the Vision)

_____

_____

_____

_____

_____

And You'll Have it!

(Write an Action Plan)

_____

_____

_____

_____

_____

Day 4
"God's Joy is My Strength, I Seek the Joy of the LORD"

There is joy to be had to those who are anchored in the Lord. He always supplies joy to His children.

His Steps...

Nehemiah 8:10 (NIV)
Nehemiah said, "Go and enjoy choice food and sweet drinks, and send some to those who have nothing prepared. This day is sacred to our Lord. Do not grieve, for the joy of the LORD is your strength."

Psalm 149:2 (NIV)
Let Israel rejoice in their Maker; let the people of Zion be glad in their King.

Isaiah 29:19 (NLT)
The humble will be filled with fresh joy from the LORD. Those who are poor will rejoice in the Holy One of Israel.

Isaiah 55:12 (AMP)
For you shall go out [from the spiritual exile caused by sin and evil into the homeland] with joy and be led forth [by your Leader, the Lord Himself, and His word] with peace; the mountains and the hills shall break forth before you into singing, and all the trees of the field shall clap their hands.

Isaiah 15:16 (NLT)
Your words are what sustain me. They bring me great joy and are my heart's delight, for I bear your name, O LORD God Almighty.

John 15:11 (NLT)
I have told you this so that you will be filled with my joy. Yes, your joy will overflow!

Romans 15:13 (NLT)
So I pray that God, who gives you hope, will keep you happy and full of peace as you believe in him. May you overflow with hope through the power of the Holy Spirit.

Hebrews 12:2 (NLT)
We do this by keeping our eyes on Jesus, on whom our faith depends from start to finish. He was willing to die a shameful death on the cross because of the joy he knew would be his afterward. Now he is seated in the place of highest honor beside God's throne in heaven.

My Steps...

Father in the name of Jesus, I thank you for this day and for your word which brings life. Thank you that you have caused me to come alive in my spirit! For the joy you have told me is my strength, for that Lord I thank you. You asked, 'why spend money on groceries that don't give us strength or do us any good'. But instead you told me to listen, and you would tell me where to go to get food that fattens the soul.

I know that means that your word is what causes us to grow and fulfills our hunger. I thank you for the word of God that lights my soul. Thank you for your words sustaining me, feeding me, bringing joy to my sorrowing heart and delighting me.

I am so very proud to bear your name, O Lord! Thank you for granting me the privilege of being called a believer. Lord for you said to me to be filled with joy and I thank you Lord that my cup runs to overflowing. Even now, I feel your presence, hallelujah!

Jesus, thank for your presence in my life. Continue to bless me and I forever give your name the praise. The glory and honor is yours is forever. In Jesus' name. Amen

When You See It...
(Write Your Vision)

_____

_____

_____

_____

_____

Then You'll Say It...
(Speak the Vision)

_____

_____

_____

_____

_____

And You'll Have it!
(Write an Action Plan)

_____

_____

_____

_____

_____

Day 5
"Seeking to Know Him More"

How do you know if you really know someone? As humans it may sometimes be difficult to determine. But with God He invites us to know Him as He already knows us.

His Steps...

Philippians 3:10-14 (NIV)
I want to know Christ and the power of his resurrection and the fellowship of sharing in his sufferings, becoming like him in his death, and so, somehow, to attain to the resurrection from the dead. Not that I have already obtained all this, or have already been made perfect, but I press on to take hold of that for which Christ Jesus took hold of me. Brothers, I do not consider myself yet to have taken hold of it. But one thing I do: Forgetting what is behind and straining toward what is ahead, I press on toward the goal to win the prize for which God has called me heavenward in Christ Jesus.

John 16:14 (NLT)
He will bring me glory by revealing to you whatever he receives from me.

My Steps...

Father God in the name of Jesus, I come just to tell you thank you. I come to let you know that I appreciate my salvation and what you did on Calvary. Lord, I desire a new walk with you, a new place in you, a new anointing upon my life. I desire to know you in a special way. Lord, as the Apostle Paul said that he might know you in the power of your resurrection, in the fellowship of your suffering, and being made conformable unto your death.

O God that is my prayer today. I want to know you more and more. I thank you because you told me that they that know their God, will be strong and do (great things) exploits.

Lord, I know that you will make the darkness light before me, and the high places, you will bring them down. I know you will and I thank you for it!

Thank you for allowing me to have an experience with you God. I want to know you like I have never known you before that your power, anointing, and might would rest upon my mind, body, and spirit, (soul and body) in this last day, in this last hour, before you come back to us. I pray that I may be able to do great things for you. I confess that it is so in Jesus' name. Amen.

(Daniel 11:32, Isaiah 42:16, Philippians 3:10)

When You See It...
(Write Your Vision)

_____
_____
_____
_____
_____

Then You'll Say It...
(Speak the Vision)

_____
_____
_____
_____
_____

And You'll Have it!
(Write an Action Plan)

_____
_____
_____
_____
_____

33

Day 6
"Seeking the Right Love"

There are many expressions of love. Some are positive and others are not. Though everyone is looking for and desires love, we must always remember that the purest, most sacrificial love we will ever know is found in the love that was demonstrated by God to us.

His Steps...

John 15:13-14 (NIV)
Greater love has no one than this that he lay down his life for his friends. You are my friends if you do what I command

Proverbs 10:12 (NIV)
Hatred stirs up dissension, but love covers over all wrongs.

John 15:10 (NIV)
If you obey my commands, you will remain in my love, just as I have obeyed my Father's commands and remain in his love

I Corinthians 8:1-6 (NIV)
Now about food sacrificed to idols: We know that we all possess knowledge. Knowledge puffs up, but love builds up. The man who thinks he knows something does not yet know as he ought to know. But the man who loves God is known by God.

I Corinthians 13

If I speak in the tongues of men and of angels, but have not love, I am only a resounding gong or a clanging cymbal. If I have the gift of prophecy and can fathom all mysteries and all knowledge, and if I have a faith that can move mountains, but have not love, I am nothing. If I give all I possess to the poor and surrender my body to the flames, but have not love, I gain nothing.

Love is patient, love is kind. It does not envy, it does not boast, it is not proud. It is not rude, it is not self-seeking, it is not easily angered, it keeps no record of wrongs. Love does not delight in evil but rejoices with the truth. It always protects, always trusts, always hopes, always perseveres.

Love never fails. But where there are prophecies, they will cease; where there are tongues, they will be stilled; where there is knowledge, it will pass away. For we know in part and we prophesy in part, but when perfection comes, the imperfect disappears. When I was a child, I talked like a child, I thought like a child, I reasoned like a child. When I became a man, I put childish ways behind me. Now we see but a poor reflection as in a mirror; then we shall see face to face. Now I know in part; then I shall know fully, even as I am fully known.

And now these three remain: faith, hope and love. But the greatest of these is love.

<u>Psalm 4:3 (NLT)</u>
You can be sure of this: The LORD has set apart
the godly for himself. The LORD will answer when I
call to him.

<u>Psalm 42:8 (NLT)</u>
Through each day the LORD pours his unfailing love
upon me, and through each night I sing his songs,
praying to God who gives me life.

<u>Psalm 89:33 (NLT)</u>
But I will never stop loving him, nor let my promise
to him fail.

My Steps...

Father in the name of Jesus, I thank you for your love. I thank you that you proved your love for the world by sending your only begotten Son, so that whosoever believes in Him would not perish, but have everlasting life. Thank you, Lord for everlasting life.

Thank you, for being good to me, for being my shelter, my joy, my peace and my hope. Everything that I can think of you have been just that for me. I thank you for life and for your word.

Thank you that you have set the redeemed apart for yourself, therefore I know you will listen to me and answer me when I call upon you. You say to me day by day that you pour out your steadfast love upon me. Through the night I sing your songs and pray to God who gives me life.

I thank you for this promise – I know you will never completely take away your loving-kindness from me nor let your promises fail. O God, thank you that you will not fail me. I know that what you have promised you will deliver! I thank you for it, and bless your name, and give your name the glory and the honor. This is my prayer in Jesus' name. Amen.
(John 3:16, Psalm 4:3, Psalm 42:8, Psalm 89:33)

Day 7
"I Pursue Wisdom in Handling Money"

Though money is not the only thing in life, it sure makes a big difference in how we live and what we are able to do. However, it is important to be re-minded that the more money we have, the more responsibility we have as well. And in order to be responsible we need God's wisdom.

His Steps...

Deuteronomy 8:18 (NIV)
But remember the LORD your God, for it is he who gives you the ability to produce wealth, and so con-firms his covenant, which he swore to your forefa-thers, as it is today.

Ecclesiastes 10:19 (KJV)
A feast is made for laughter, and wine maketh merry: but money answereth all things.

Ecclesiastes 5:10 (NIV)
Whoever loves money never has money enough; whoever loves wealth is never satisfied with his in-come. This too is meaningless.

Joshua 1:8 (NIV)
Do not let this Book of the Law depart from your mouth; meditate on it day and night, so that you

may be careful to do everything written in it. Then you will be prosperous and successful.

Philippians 4:19 (NLT)
And this same God who takes care of me will supply all your needs from his glorious riches, which have been given to us in Christ Jesus.

Matthew 6:30-33 (NLT)
And if God cares so wonderfully for flowers that are here today and gone tomorrow, won't he more surely care for you? You have so little faith!
"So don't worry about having enough food or drink or clothing. Why be like the pagans who are so deeply concerned about these things? Your heavenly Father already knows all your needs, and he will give you all you need from day to day if you live for him and make the Kingdom of God your primary concern.

Luke 6:38 (NLT)
If you give, you will receive. Your gift will return to you in full measure, pressed down, shaken together to make room for more, and running over. Whatever measure you use in giving—large or small—it will be used to measure what is given back to you."

2 Corinthians 9:6 (NLT)
Remember this—a farmer who plants only a few seeds will get a small crop. But the one who plants generously will get a generous crop.

Malachi 3:8-12 (NIV)

"Will a man rob God? Yet you rob me.

"But you ask, 'How do we rob you?'

"In tithes and offerings. You are under a curse (the whole nation of you), because you are robbing me. Bring the whole tithe into the storehouse, that there may be food in my house. Test me in this," says the LORD Almighty, "and see if I will not throw open the floodgates of heaven and pour out so much blessing that you will not have room enough for it. I will prevent pests from devouring your crops, and the vines in your fields will not cast their fruit," says the LORD Almighty. "Then all the nations will call you blessed, for yours will be a delightful land," says the LORD Almighty.

My Steps...

Father in the name of Jesus, I thank you for this day of prayer. I am grateful to know that when I need anything, I can find it in you. I thank you for your word. You promised to supply all my needs according to your riches in glory, by Christ Jesus.

Jesus you promised that you would bless us and make us the head and not the tail. You promised to make us lenders and not borrowers. Lord Jesus, I confess I have plenty of money. I confess Lord, I'll never be broke another day of my life. I confess as I believe in you and walk in your ways money shall come, dollars shall come (daily and weekly) into my possession.

O God, material things will help sustain me. Help me to go forward in the ministry, in the gospel, in the work of the Lord. I shall not want for any good thing that will permit me to carry on the work, of my Savior.

Lord I confess and believe it in my heart. As I speak it through my lips right now I can see it through the eyes of faith and I know it is happening for me right now! These and other blessings, I receive and accept and claim in Jesus' name. Amen.
(Deut. 8, Job, Matthew 6)

When You See It...
(Write Your Vision)

_____

_____

_____

_____

_____

Then You'll Say It...
(Speak the Vision)

_____

_____

_____

_____

_____

And You'll Have it!
(Write an Action Plan)

_____

_____

_____

_____

_____

Day 8
"I Earnestly Contend for Patience"

Who has not said at one time or another, "Lord, give me patience." It is without a doubt one of the most necessary attributes in life. In order to flow in an attitude of patience, there must be a decision made each day to do so. A patient spirit is not too far out of reach if we contend for it daily.

His Steps...

James 1:3-4 (NIV)
Because you know that the testing of your faith develops perseverance. Perseverance must finish its work so that you may be mature and complete, not lacking anything.

James 5:7-8 (NLT)
Dear brothers and sisters, you must be patient as you wait for the Lord's return. Consider the farmers who eagerly look for the rains in the fall and in the spring. They patiently wait for the precious harvest to ripen. You, too, must be patient. And take courage, for the coming of the Lord is near.

Galatians 6:9 (KJV)
And let us not be weary in well doing: for in due season we shall reap, if we faint not.

Hebrews 10:36 (KJV)
For ye have need of patience, that, after ye have done the will of God, ye might receive the promise.

Hebrews 12:1 (KJV)
Wherefore seeing we also are compassed about with so great a cloud of witnesses, let us lay aside every weight, and the sin which doth so easily beset us, and let us run with patience the race that is set before us,

My Steps...

Father in the name of Jesus, I thank you for patience. For when the way is rough your patience has a chance to grow in me. I thank you for that. You said to be patient and take courage for your coming is near. I thank you and confess patience in my spirit. I confess that I have patience, and I allow patience to have its perfect work in my life from this day forward, in Jesus' name. Amen (James 1:3, James 5:8)

When You See It...
(Write Your Vision)

_____

_____

_____

_____

_____

Then You'll Say It...
(Speak the Vision)

_____

_____

_____

_____

_____

And You'll Have it!
(Write an Action Plan)

_____

_____

_____

_____

_____

Day 9
"Peace is a Must"

Peace is not an option. Jesus left His own brand of peace for every believer. But in order to have true peace there must be a clear decision of obedience to God and love toward others. Determine today that you will have peace!

His Steps...

Philippians 4:6-7 (NIV)
Do not be anxious about anything, but in everything, by prayer and petition, with thanksgiving, present your requests to God. And the peace of God, which transcends all understanding, will guard your hearts and your minds in Christ Jesus.

Psalms 122:7-8 (KJV)
Peace be within thy walls, and prosperity within thy palaces. For my brethren and companions' sakes, I will now say, Peace be within thee.

Proverbs 3:2, 17 (KJV)
For length of days, and long life, and peace, shall they add to thee.

Her ways are ways of pleasantness, and all her paths are peace.

Isaiah 54: 13-14 (KJV)
And all thy children shall be taught of the LORD; and great shall be the peace of thy children. In righteousness shalt thou be established: thou shalt be far from oppression; for thou shalt not fear: and from terror; for it shall not come near thee.

Romans 16:20 (KJV)
And the God of peace shall bruise Satan under your feet shortly. The grace of our Lord Jesus Christ be with you. Amen.

John 14:27 (NIV)
Peace I leave with you; my peace I give you. I do not give to you as the world gives. Do not let your hearts be troubled and do not be afraid.

Leviticus 26:6-8 (NIV)
" 'I will grant peace in the land, and you will lie down and no one will make you afraid. I will remove savage beasts from the land, and the sword will not pass through your country. You will pursue your enemies, and they will fall by the sword before you. Five of you will chase a hundred, and a hundred of you will chase ten thousand, and your enemies will fall by the sword before you.

Colossians 3:15 (NLT)
And let the peace that comes from Christ rule in your hearts. For as members of one body you are all called to live in peace. And always be thankful.

Psalm 4:8 (NLT)
I will lie down in peace and sleep, for you alone, O LORD, will keep me safe.

My Steps...

Father in the name of Jesus, I pray that as I read your word that there are others who are doing the same thing. I pray for other today. I pray that if there is a need of peace that peace shall be theirs. I pray for peace in their spirit, mind and soul. I thank you for the manifestation of peace for them right now.

Thank you for the promise of great peace to our children and that you give peace to their souls. We know that if we let Christ be Lord in these affairs that we will experience gladness and so will others. I appreciate that your word says that to us. I believe and confess that I will lie down and sleep for though I am alone, you will keep me safe.

Thank you for your word, in Jesus' name. Amen. (Romans 14:18, Psalms 4:7)

When You See It...
(Write Your Vision)

_____

_____

_____

_____

_____

Then You'll Say It...
(Speak the Vision)

_____

_____

_____

_____

_____

And You'll Have it!
(Write an Action Plan)

_____

_____

_____

_____

_____

Day 10
"Forgetting Things Behind Me"

Everyone has had someone hurt or disappoint them. Sadly, that can be expected at one time or another. But even more sad than that is when the hurt is not forgiven or forgotten.

There are even times when we ourselves have situations and things for which we must forgive ourselves. The key in either case is to 'put the past in the past' and leave it there. If this is done you will be able to see a whole new outlook on life!

His Steps...

Philippians 3:13-14 (NLT)
No, dear brothers and sisters, I am still not all I should be, but I am focusing all my energies on this one thing: Forgetting the past and looking forward to what lies ahead, I strain to reach the end of the race and receive the prize for which God, through Christ Jesus, is calling us up to heaven.

Isaiah 26:12-14 (NLT)
LORD, you will grant us peace, for all we have accomplished is really from you. O LORD our God, others have ruled us, but we worship you alone. Those we served before are dead and gone. Never again will they return! You attacked them and destroyed them, and they are long forgotten.

Isaiah 43:10 (NLT)

"But you are my witnesses, O Israel!" says the LORD. "And you are my servant. You have been chosen to know me, believe in me, and understand that I alone am God. There is no other God; there never has been and never will be.

2 Corinthians 5:17 (NLT)

What this means is that those who become Christians become new persons. They are not the same anymore, for the old life is gone. A new life has begun!

My Steps...

Father, I thank you for my soul magnifies you! Thank you for keeping me, keeping my mind, and keeping my feet on the right path, my hands from shedding innocent blood. Thank you for keeping my spirit and for giving me the mind to reach out to your Son and to my fellow man. Thank you for what I am experiencing in this journey with you.

I thank you that my cup is running over and that the Holy Spirit is visiting me. I bless you and glorify you right now in this very hour. I confess and believe every scripture I read today. I confess that victory is mine and that everything I have prayed today is done, in Jesus' name. Amen.

When You See It...
(Write Your Vision)

_____

_____

_____

_____

_____

Then You'll Say It...
(Speak the Vision)

_____

_____

_____

_____

_____

And You'll Have it!
(Write an Action Plan)

_____

_____

_____

_____

_____

Day 11
"I Must Overcome My Doubts"

Doubt is a manifestation of fear. And since fear is the faith canceller. Doubt is the signal to every believer that fear is present.

In order to truly overcome doubt you must identify, where fear is coming from. Then when identified, confession and belief of the Word will zap that doubt right out!

His Steps...

Psalm 138:8 (NLT)
The LORD will work out his plans for my life—for your faithful love, O LORD, endures forever. Don't abandon me, for you made me.

Hebrews 10:23 (NLT)
Without wavering, let us hold tightly to the hope we say we have, for God can be trusted to keep his promise.

John 8:31-32 (NLT)
Jesus said to the people who believed in him, "You are truly my disciples if you keep obeying my teachings. And you will know the truth, and the truth will set you free."

1 Chronicles 16:21 (NLT)
Yet he did not let anyone oppress them. He warned kings on their behalf:

Acts 1:8 (NLT)
But when the Holy Spirit has come upon you, you will receive power and will tell people about me everywhere—in Jerusalem, throughout Judea, in Samaria, and to the ends of the earth."

1 Corinthians 2:14 (NLT)
But people who aren't Christians can't understand these truths from God's Spirit. It all sounds foolish to them because only those who have the Spirit can understand what the Spirit means.

John 10:24 (KJV)
Then came the Jews round about him, and said unto him, How long dost thou make us to doubt? If thou be the Christ, tell us plainly.

Matthew 14:31 (KJV)
And immediately Jesus stretched forth his hand, and caught him, and said unto him, O thou of little faith, wherefore didst thou doubt?

My Steps...

Lord Jesus, I thank you for keeping me with a mind to trust you. You have kept me with a mind of faith in the word. Lord, I know that it is the enemy's job to somewhere in my lifetime, on this journey with you, to bring doubt and unbelief; but you have always encouraged me. You said if I could, believe all things are possible to me.

I thank you for knowing that if I can believe and doubt in my heart of all those things I have asked you for, and all the petitions that I have placed before you, they are mine. You have told me that I shall know the truth, and the truth will set you free. Lord I thank you for truth. You told me in the word that you desire truth in the inward parts.

Thank you Lord for truth, that you have cast out all doubt, and you have allowed it to happen through the word. Wherever I go you use me to tell others and to spread the gospel like a sweet perfume. Lord, I thank you that you will work out your plan for my life. Your loving kindness continues forever. Lord I know you will not leave me. I ask you to help me stand and when needed to regroup. Help me to read and eat the word. Help me to pray and I can overcome the enemy of doubt to move on in victory. I thank you for it now. Hallelujah! Hallelujah! Hallelujah! I thank you that it is done in Jesus' name. Amen. [John 8:31-32]

When You See It...
(Write Your Vision)

_____

_____

_____

_____

_____

Then You'll Say It...
(Speak the Vision)

_____

_____

_____

_____

_____

And You'll Have it!
(Write an Action Plan)

_____

_____

_____

_____

_____

Day 12
"Turning My Failures into Success"

When it comes to success and failure the real question becomes how to determine when a failure has really taken place. Since life teaches us things that look like failures today, may have been triumphs unrecognized. The greatest asset you have when turning your perceived failures into successes is how you view the control God has of your life.

His Steps...

Psalm 37:23-24 [NLT]
The steps of the godly are directed by the LORD. He delights in every detail of their lives. Though they stumble, they will not fall, for the LORD holds them by the hand.

Galatians 6:9 [KJV]
And let us not be weary in well doing: for in due season we shall reap, if we faint not.

Joshua 1:8 [KJV]
This book of the law shall not depart out of thy mouth; but thou shalt meditate therein day and night, that thou mayest observe to do according to all that is written therein: for then thou shalt make thy way prosperous, and then thou shalt have good success.

Jude 20 [KJV]
But ye, beloved, building up yourselves on your most holy faith, praying in the Holy Ghost.

61

My Steps...

Father in the name of Jesus, I thank you for your presence. I thank you for what I feel in my spirit and for the word. You told me that the steps of a good man are ordered of the Lord and I thank you for ordering and directing my steps. I thank you for the direction my path is taking for I know I will not fail.

I thank you for your word says you will hold me with your hand, and I thank you. You encourage me by telling me not to be weary in well doing, for in due season I would reap if I don't faint.

Thank you for your blessings. Thank you for success. Thank you for putting failure under my feet. Thank you that the past is under the blood and success is all that I have before me to enjoy because I am learning to walk by faith. Thank you for all these things in Jesus' name I pray. Amen. [Psalm 37:24, Galatians 6:9, Joshua 1:8]

When You See It...
(Write Your Vision)

_____

_____

_____

_____

_____

Then You'll Say It...
(Speak the Vision)

_____

_____

_____

_____

_____

And You'll Have it!
(Write an Action Plan)

_____

_____

_____

_____

_____

Day 13
"I Will Ask God for His Direction"

The real issue is not whether God will give direction when you ask. It is rather will you obey when He speaks.

His Steps...

Hebrews 3:7-10 (NLT)
That is why the Holy Spirit says, "Today you must listen to his voice. Don't harden your hearts against him as Israel did when they rebelled, when they tested God's patience in the wilderness.

There your ancestors tried my patience, even though they saw my miracles for forty years. So I was angry with them, and I said, 'Their hearts always turn away from me. They refuse to do what I tell them.'

Romans 12:1-2 (NLT)
And so, dear brothers and sisters, I plead with you to give your bodies to God. Let them be a living and holy sacrifice—the kind he will accept. When you think of what he has done for you, is this too much to ask?

Don't copy the behavior and customs of this world, but let God transform you into a new person by changing the way you think. Then you will know what God wants you to do, and you will know how good and pleasing and perfect his will really is.

My Steps...

Father in the name of Jesus, I thank you for this day. I thank you for being good to me. Thank you for being the God that you are, for bringing me through every storm, every valley, every hill, every hamlet, I thank you for it.

I thank you for you said that the children of Israel couldn't make it to the place of rest because they didn't make the right decision. They didn't trust you and lean on your word to them, which caused them to wander in the wilderness for 40 years.

Lord, I pray that you will help me make right decisions so that I will not lose any blessings that belong to me. Help me Lord! Help me to acknowledge you and look to you. Help me keep my flesh under subjection. I also confess that I will not think more highly of myself than I ought. I will always recognize that without you I can do nothing. I am nothing. But with you by my side I can run through troops and leap over walls.

With you in my life, every step I take, every move I make will be a fruitful one, because I have taken you as my leader and my guide, as my God, as my protector, my father, my everything. Thank you Lord for what I feel right now. My cup is running over and tears of joy flow my soul. Lord continue to bless, in Jesus name. Amen.

When You See It...
(Write Your Vision)

_____

_____

_____

_____

_____

Then You'll Say It...
(Speak the Vision)

_____

_____

_____

_____

_____

And You'll Have it!
(Write an Action Plan)

_____

_____

_____

_____

_____

Day 14
"Lord Teach Me to Pray"

When a person desires an effective prayer life. What he or she is really asking for is a sincere ability to communicate with God and He with them. If this is your prayer, I promise that He wants nothing more than to answer it!

His Steps...

Psalm 119:130 (KJV)
The entrance of Your words gives light; It gives understanding to the simple.

2 Samuel 7:18 (KJV)
Nevertheless a lad saw them, and told Absalom: but they went both of them away quickly, and came to a man's house in Bahurim, which had a well in his court; whither they went down.

Matthew 6:9-13 (KJV)
After this manner therefore pray ye: Our Father which art in heaven, Hallowed be thy name. Thy kingdom come, Thy will be done in earth, as it is in heaven. Give us this day our daily bread. And forgive us our debts, as we forgive our debtors. And lead us not into temptation, but deliver us from evil: For thine is the kingdom, and the power, and the glory, for ever. Amen.

Nehemiah 1:5-11 (KJV)

And said, I beseech thee, O LORD God of heaven, the great and terrible God, that keepeth covenant and mercy for them that love him and observe his commandments: Let thine ear now be attentive, and thine eyes open, that thou mayest hear the prayer of thy servant, which I pray before thee now, day and night, for the children of Israel thy servants, and confess the sins of the children of Israel, which we have sinned against thee: both I and my father's house have sinned. We have dealt very corruptly against thee, and have not kept the commandments, nor the statutes, nor the judgments, which thou commandedst thy servant Moses. Remember, I beseech thee, the word that thou commandedst thy servant Moses, saying, If ye transgress, I will scatter you abroad among the nations: But if ye turn unto me, and keep my commandments, and do them; though there were of you cast out unto the uttermost part of the heaven, yet will I gather them from thence, and will bring them unto the place that I have chosen to set my name there. Now these are thy servants and thy people, whom thou hast redeemed by thy great power, and by thy strong hand. O LORD, I beseech thee, let now thine ear be attentive to the prayer of thy servant, and to the prayer of thy servants, who desire to fear thy name: and prosper, I pray thee, thy servant this day, and grant him mercy in the sight of this man. For I was the king's cupbearer.

Ecclesiastes 2:26 (NLT)

God gives wisdom, knowledge, and joy to those who please him. But if a sinner becomes wealthy, God takes the wealth away and gives it to those who please him. Even this, however, is meaningless, like chasing the wind.

Luke 21:15 (KJV)

For I will give you a mouth and wisdom which all your adversaries will not be able to contradict or resist.

John 6:45 (KJV)

It is written in the prophets, "And they shall all be taught by God. Therefore everyone who has heard and learned, from the Father comes to Me.

My Steps...

Father in the name of Jesus, I thank you for this sweet time of prayer. I thank you for the chance to talk to you and for giving me the understanding that prayer is communicating with you, making my needs and requests known to you; giving thanks, praise and adoration to you. You are the Sovereign God who is merciful to me.

Thank you Lord for allowing me to come and talk to you. I am grateful that I can tell you intimate secrets and tell you things that I can't tell anyone else. I can tell you things that I can't tell my parents, siblings or friends. But I can tell you because you told me in your word that if anyone lacks wisdom, let him ask you, and you promised to give us wisdom, and would not rebuke us for asking for it. Let your kingdom come; let your will be done in this earth as it is in heaven. I know in Heaven there it is peace; there it is joy and Holy Spirit

We know in heaven the people are rejoicing. Lord, so much confusion, so much hatred, envy, malice, strife, so much wickedness and perversion, so much of the wrong things happening on earth. Let your kingdom come; let your will be done, right now. In Jesus name I pray, I believe you for it. Amen.

When You See It...
(Write Your Vision)

_____
_____
_____
_____
_____

Then You'll Say It...
(Speak the Vision)

_____
_____
_____
_____
_____

And You'll Have it!
(Write an Action Plan)

_____
_____
_____
_____

Day 15
"Praying God's Word"

The Word of God is powerful and full of life. As you pray, you are releasing the very life-giving power of God into the atmosphere, which is how God Himself created everything you see today!

His Steps...

John 14:14 (NLT)
Yes, ask anything in my name, and I will do it!

Psalm 55:17-18 (AMP)
Evening and morning and at noon will I utter my complaint and moan and sigh, and He will hear my voice. He has redeemed my life in peace from the battle that was against me [so that none came near me], for they were many who strove with me.

Isaiah 26:3 (NLT)
You will keep in perfect peace all who trust in you, whose thoughts are fixed on you!

I Corinthians 14:4 (NLT)
A person who speaks in tongues is strengthened personally in the Lord, but one who speaks a word of prophecy strengthens the entire church.

Jude 20 (KJV)
But ye, beloved, building up yourselves on your most holy faith, praying in the Holy Ghost,

My Steps...

Father in the name of Jesus, I thank you for teaching me how to pray. I am grateful for the revelation that I can pray your word. I can because Jeremiah said that you watch over your word, and that you move quickly to perform your Word. Lord, I thank you for letting me know whenever I apply the word; I will see action because you stated it in your word. Your word is sure and will never fail. You said that heaven and earth shall pass away but your word would not.

Lord, thank you for the guarantee that you would make heaven and earth vanish, before any of your word would fail. What a guarantee! Lord, you promised that as your word went out of your mouth it shall not return to you void, but it shall accomplish that which you sent it, and shall prosper in the thing where you sent it.

Lord Jesus I thank you that your word is going to get the job done. I thank you, Lord that I am learning to pray according to your will, according to your word. I know that's a guaranteed answer to prayer. Thank you for it! Amen.

When You See It...
(Write Your Vision)

Then You'll Say It...
(Speak the Vision)

And You'll Have it!
(Write an Action Plan)

Day 16
"I Will Obtain Strength to Soar as an Eagle"

His plan is outlined in His Word, but His personal desire for your life is revealed as you spend time with Him. As you do you will discover all the wonderful things God has in store for your life!

His Steps...

<u>Ezekiel 36:37 (NLT)</u>
"This is what the Sovereign LORD says: I am ready to hear Israel's prayers for these blessings, and I am ready to grant them their requests.

<u>Isaiah 40:31 (KJV)</u>
But they that wait upon the LORD shall renew their strength; they shall mount up with wings as eagles; they shall run, and not be weary; and they shall walk, and not faint.

<u>Isaiah 62:6-7 (NLT)</u>
O Jerusalem, I have posted watchmen on your walls; they will pray to the LORD day and night for the fulfillment of his promises. Take no rest, all you who pray. Give the LORD no rest until he makes Jerusalem the object of praise throughout the earth.

<u>Phiiliipans 4:13 (KJV)</u>
I can do all things thriugh Christ which strengtheneth me.

Acts 8:17-19 (NLT)
Then Peter and John laid their hands upon these believers, and they received the Holy Spirit. When Simon saw that the Holy Spirit was given when the apostles placed their hands upon people's heads, he offered money to buy this power. "Let me have this power, too," he exclaimed, "so that when I lay my hands on people, they will receive the Holy Spirit!"

Acts 9:10-17 (NLT)
Now there was a believer in Damascus named Ananias. The Lord spoke to him in a vision, calling, "Ananias!" "Yes, Lord!" he replied. The Lord said, "Go over to Straight Street, to the house of Judas. When you arrive, ask for Saul of Tarsus. He is praying to me right now. I have shown him a vision of a man named Ananias coming in and laying his hands on him so that he can see again." "But Lord," exclaimed Ananias, "I've heard about the terrible things this man has done to the believers in Jerusalem! And we hear that he is authorized by the leading priests to arrest every believer in Damascus."But the Lord said, "Go and do what I say. For Saul is my chosen instrument to take my message to the Gentiles and to kings, as well as to the people of Israel. And I will show him how much he must suffer for me." So Ananias went and found Saul. He laid his hands on him and said, "Brother Saul, the Lord Jesus, who appeared to you on the road, has sent me so that you may get your sight back and be filled with the Holy Spirit."

My Steps...

Father in the name of Jesus, I thank you that my soul is mellowing with the time I am praying, reading the word and meditating on your promises. O God my soul loves and magnifies you. God I see you ate work in my life. I see your word turning my life around, strengthening me, encouraging my life, healing my spirit, healing my wounds, healing the disappointments, the heartaches, the miseries, the loneliness and the frustrations. Thank you Lord that I can see your word at work.

You said you would give me another comforter. He will never leave me and I thank you Lord that you have sent the Holy Spirit and even now I feel Him comforting and ministering to me. I feel my soul rejoicing because I feel the Holy Spirit upon my soul right now. Lord, I thank you for the word. I know the word is going to do all that it promises to do, all that is spoken of to do, will be done in and through my life. This is my prayer in Jesus' name. Amen.

When You See It...
(Write Your Vision)

_____

_____

_____

_____

_____

Then You'll Say It...
(Speak the Vision)

_____

_____

_____

_____

And You'll Have it!
(Write an Action Plan)

_____

_____

_____

_____

_____

Day 17
"I Will Forget the Failures of the Past"

It is vitally important that one doesn't get booged down with the failures of the past. But forge ahead learnig from the mistakes of the past.

His Steps...

Matthew 26:44 (NLT)
So he went back to pray a third time, saying the same things again.

Matthew 18:19 (NLT)
"I also tell you this: If two of you agree down here on earth concerning anything you ask, my Father in heaven will do it for you.

Phiilipians 3:13-14 (KJV)
Brethren, I count not myself to have apprehended: but this one thing I do, forgetting those things which are behind, and reaching forth unto those things which are before, I press toward the mark for the prize of the high calling of God in Christ Jesus.

2 Corinthians 5:17 (KJV)
Therefore if any man be in Christ, he is a new creature: old things are passed away; behold, all things are become new.

2 Corinthians 12:8 (NLT)
Three different times I begged the Lord to take it away.

Luke 18:2-8 (NLT)
"There was a judge in a certain city," he said, "who was a godless man with great contempt for everyone. A widow of that city came to him repeatedly, appealing for justice against someone who had harmed her. The judge ignored her for a while, but eventually she wore him out. `I fear neither God nor man,' he said to himself, `but this woman is driving me crazy. I'm going to see that she gets justice, because she is wearing me out with her constant requests!' "

Then the Lord said, "Learn a lesson from this evil judge. Even he rendered a just decision in the end, so don't you think God will surely give justice to his chosen people who plead with him day and night? Will he keep putting them off? I tell you, he will grant justice to them quickly! But when I, the Son of Man, return, how many will I find who have faith?"

My Steps...

Father in the name of Jesus, I thank you for the word. You said that many are called but few are chosen. Thank you for the calling. Thank you for calling, choosing, and using me in these last days. Lord Jesus, you promised, O God, that you would be with me, and that we could make it through any storm; and Paul reminded us that we could say that we know all things work together for the good to them that love the Lord and are the called.

O God thank you for the call according to your purpose. I am one of the called, but I know that I have not been called for my purpose, but for yours. I have been called to do your will and I thank you for calling me. I pray that you will help me to keep an eye on my flesh. You called, anointed and appointed me. Thank you Jesus. I thank you for it. Amen.

When You See It...
(Write Your Vision)

_____

_____

_____

_____

_____

Then You'll Say It...
(Speak the Vision)

_____

_____

_____

_____

And You'll Have it!

(Write an Action Plan)

_____

_____

_____

_____

_____

Day 18
"I Will Respond to the Call Of God"

As you spend time with the Lord in prayer, it is certain that He will begin to speak to you concerning His plan of service for you to others. The best advice anyone can give to you is to heed His call and surrender to Him in this area. Because it will truly be the only place you will find complete fulfillment and peace.

His Steps...

Isaiah 55:1-2 (KJV)
Ho, every one that thirsteth, come ye to the waters, and he that hath no money; come ye, buy, and eat; yea, come, buy wine and milk without money and without price. Wherefore do ye spend money for that which is not bread? and your labour for that which satisfieth not? hearken diligently unto me, and eat ye that which is good, and let your soul delight itself in fatness.

John 6:35 (NLT)
Jesus replied, "I am the bread of life. No one who comes to me will ever be hungry again. Those who believe in me will never thirst.

.

Romans 8:28 (KJV)
And we know that all things work together for good to them that love God, to them who are the called according to his purpose.

My Steps...

.

Father in the name of Jesus, I thank you for the word. You said that many are called but few are chosen. Thank you for the calling. Thank you for choosing and using me in these last days. Lord Jesus, you promised, O God, that you would be with me, and that we could make it through any storm. Paul reminded us we could say that we know all things work together for the good to them that love you and are the called. O God, thank you for the call according to your purpose. I know I am one of the called. But I understand that I have not been called for my purpose but for yours. I have been called to do your will. I pray that you will help me to keep an eye on my flesh. You called me, you anointed me, you appointed me, and I thank you for it, in Jesus' name. Amen.

When You See It...
(Write Your Vision)

_____

_____

_____

_____

_____

Then You'll Say It...
(Speak the Vision)

_____

_____

_____

_____

And You'll Have it!
(Write an Action Plan)

_____

_____

_____

_____

Day 19
"I Will Wait On the Lord"

It is a challenge to wait, especially when you see no evidence that things are going in your direction. But be assured that God is worth waiting for and He has yet to be late and has always kept His promise.

His Steps...

Proverbs 3:6 (NLT)
Seek his will in all you do, and he will direct your paths.

Matthew 11:28-29 (NLT)
Then Jesus said, "Come to me, all of you who are weary and carry heavy burdens, and I will give you rest. Take my yoke upon you. Let me teach you, because I am humble and gentle, and you will find rest for your souls.

Psalm 27:14 (NLT)
Wait patiently for the LORD. Be brave and courageous. Yes, wait patiently for the LORD.

Psalm 37:34 (NLT)
Don't be impatient for the LORD to act! Travel steadily along his path. He will honor you, giving you the land. You will see the wicked destroyed.

My Steps...

Father in the name of Jesus, I thank you for another day. I thank you for teaching me to wait on you and how not to become impatient, but to wait for you to sustain me and for you to bring me through. You told me not to be impatient, but to wait for you to come and save me. You want me to be brave, stouthearted and courageous. As I wait on the Lord, I know he will help me. You don't want me to be impatient for the Lord to act, but to keep traveling along your pathway, and in due season he will honor me with every blessing and I will see the wicked destroyed. Thank you for it Jesus. I accept it by faith. Amen.

When You See It...
(Write Your Vision)

_____
_____
_____
_____
_____

Then You'll Say It...
(Speak the Vision)

_____
_____
_____
_____
_____

And You'll Have it!
(Write an Action Plan)

_____
_____
_____
_____
_____

Day 20
"I Will Make Myself Happy"

I am most happy when _____
_____
_____
_____
_____

His Steps...

Acts 26:2 (KJV)
I think myself happy, king Agrippa, because I shall answer for myself this day before thee touching all the things whereof I am accused of the Jews:

Proverbs 16:20 (KJV)
He that handleth a matter wisely shall find good: and whoso trusteth in the LORD, happy is he.

Proverbs 14:21 (KJV)
He that despiseth his neighbour sinneth: but he that hath mercy on the poor, happy is he.

Romans 14:22 (KJV)
Hast thou faith? Have it to thyself before God. Happy is he that condemneth not himself in that thing which he alloweth.

James 5:11 (KJV)
Behold, we count them happy which endure. Ye have heard of the patience of Job, and have seen the end of the Lord; that the Lord is very pitiful, and of tender mercy.

Psalm 30:5 (NLT)
His anger lasts for a moment, but his favor lasts a lifetime! Weeping may go on all night,   but joy comes with the morning.

Psalm 16:11 (NLT)
You will show me the way of life, granting me the joy of your presence and the pleasures of living with you forever.

Jeremiah 15:16 (NLT)
Your words are what sustain me. They bring me great joy and are my heart's delight, for I bear your name, O LORD God Almighty.

Isaiah 51:11 (NLT)
Those who have been ransomed by the LORD will return to Jerusalem, singing songs of everlasting joy. Sorrow and mourning will disappear, and they will be overcome with joy and gladness.

Nehemiah 8:10 (KJV)
Then he said unto them, Go your way, eat the fat, and drink the sweet, and send portions unto them for whom nothing is prepared: for this day is holy unto our LORD: neither be ye sorry; for the joy of the LORD is your strength.

John 15:11 (KJV)
These things have I spoken unto you, that my joy might remain in you, and that your joy might be full.

My Steps...

Father in the name of Jesus, I thank you for putting your word and anointing upon me. Thank you that I am gaining strength in the word. Thank you for the anointing that is upon my life. Thank you for being my leader, my guide and my director. Thank you Lord that you have delivered me from the hands of the enemy, who tried his best to destroy me. Thank you, bless me and keep me close to you, in Jesus name, Amen.

When You See It...
(Write Your Vision)

_____

_____

_____

_____

_____

Then You'll Say It...
(Speak the Vision)

_____

_____

_____

_____

And You'll Have it!
(Write an Action Plan)

_____

_____

_____

_____

_____

Day 21
"Deliverance Belongs to Me"

Deliverance is available to every believer. Whatever issue you are facing, it has been and will never be too difficult for God to handle. Just bring it to Him and He will deliver you.

His Steps...

Psalm 106:8 (NLT)
Even so, he saved them—to defend the honor of his name and to demonstrate his mighty power

Matthew 18:14 (NLT)
In the same way, it is not my heavenly Father's will that even one of these little ones should perish.

Luke 4:18-19 (KJV)
The Spirit of the Lord is upon me, because he hath anointed me to preach the gospel to the poor; he hath sent me to heal the broken-hearted, to preach deliverance to the captives, and recovering of sight to the blind, so to set at liberty them that are bruised. To preach the acceptable year of the Lord.

Ephesians 2:4-5 (NLT)
But God is so rich in mercy, and he loved us so very much, that even while we were dead because of our sins, he gave us life when he raised Christ from the dead. (It is only by God's special favor that you have been saved!)

<u>2 Timothy 1:9 (NLT)</u>
It is God who saved us and chose us to live a holy life. He did this not because we deserved it, but because that was his plan long before the world began—to show his love and kindness to us through Christ Jesus.

My Steps...

Father in the name of Jesus, I come to tell you thank you for deliverance and for letting me know that I need salvation and that it is available to me. And when I need deliverance you make sure I know it is available to me. You said that though you saved us to defend the honor of your name and to demonstrate your power to the entire world and that salvation comes from God, and joy you give to all people.

But you are so rich in mercy, you love us so much, that even though we were spiritually dead and doomed by our sins, you gave us back our lives again, when you raised Christ from the dead. Only by your undeserved favor have we ever been saved. Father, thank you for this sacrifice. Mold and bless me is my prayer, in Jesus name. Amen.

When You See It...
(Write Your Vision)

_____

_____

_____

_____

Then You'll Say It...
(Speak the Vision)

_____

_____

_____

_____

And You'll Have it!
(Write an Action Plan)

_____

_____

_____

_____

_____

Day 22
"God's Perfect Love Conquers Fear"

It is His love that is the winning ingredient to conquering fear. It was that love that led Jesus to the cross and it is that same love that you can depend on when you encounter any circumstance that will come your way. Fear can't stand against the love that God has for you.

His Steps...

2 Timothy 1:7 (KJV)
For God hath not given us the spirit of fear; but of power, and of love, and of a sound mind.

1 John 4:8 (KJV)
He that loveth not knoweth not God; for God is love.

Psalm 27:1 (KJV)
The LORD is my light and my salvation; whom shall I fear? the LORD is the strength of my life; of whom shall I be afraid?

My Steps...

Father in the name of Jesus, I come at this moment to thank you for your perfect love. Thank you for the word, for I know that the Lord is my light and my salvation (He protects me from danger) whom shall I fear. I thank you for your perfect love, and I know that you truly love me, and that you care for me. Lord Jesus, whatever you do to me and for me is because of your love and you are concerned about your creation. Thank you for my knowing that there is perfect love toward mankind. Thank you Lord for my experience. Lord I feel your loving arms wrapped around me, protecting me, as a father protects his child. I thank you for the blessed hope and for it happening in my spirit right now! In Jesus' name, Amen.

When You See It...
(Write Your Vision)

_____
_____
_____
_____
_____

Then You'll Say It...
(Speak the Vision)

_____
_____
_____
_____
_____

And You'll Have it!
(Write an Action Plan)

_____
_____
_____
_____
_____

Day 23
"There are Special Promises for the Young at Heart"

Write a prayer for today's youth.

_____

_____

_____

_____

_____

His Steps...

1 Timothy 4:12 (NLT)
Don't let anyone think less of you because you are young. Be an example to all believers in what you teach, in the way you live, in your love, your faith, and your purity.

2 Timothy 3:14-15 (NLT)
But you must remain faithful to the things you have been taught. You know they are true, for you know you can trust those who taught you. [15]You have been taught the holy Scriptures from childhood, and they have given you the wisdom to receive the salvation that comes by trusting in Christ Jesus.

Psalm 119:9 (KJV)
Wherewithal shall a young man cleanse his way? by taking heed thereto according to thy word.

My Steps...

Lord Jesus, I come to tell you that I truly thank you for the power of your word. Thank you Lord, for you have reached out to many of the children. You asked a question, 'how can a young man stay pure?' The answer is by reading your word, and following its rules. I must continue to believe the things I have been taught because they are true. Happy is the man with a levelheaded son. Lord, I just thank you for our youth. I know that you are going to save, heal and deliver them. I thank you for being able to experience your love. I thank you for all blessings in Jesus' name. This is my prayer. Amen.

When You See It...
(Write Your Vision)

_____
_____
_____
_____
_____

Then You'll Say It...
(Speak the Vision)

_____
_____
_____
_____
_____

And You'll Have it!
(Write an Action Plan)

_____
_____
_____
_____
_____

Day 24
'When Bad Things Happen to Good People"

We have all heard or seen situations where we have thought to ourselves, 'How could that have happened to them?' Or maybe we have said this of ourselves when trouble strikes. But we can know that He is always there to comfort us.

His Steps...

Genesis 50:20 (KJV)
But as for you, ye thought evil against me; but God meant it unto good, to bring to pass, as it is this day, to save much people alive.

Esther 4:13 (KJV)
Then Mordecai commanded to answer Esther, Think not with thyself that thou shalt escape in the king's house, more than all the Jews.

James 1:2-4 (NLT)
Dear brothers and sisters, whenever trouble comes your way, let it be an opportunity for joy. For when your faith is tested, your endurance has a chance to grow. So let it grow, for when your endurance is fully developed, you will be strong in character and ready for anything.

Acts 10:46 (NLT)

And there could be no doubt about it, for they heard them speaking in tongues and praising God.

Hebrews 12:5-6 (NLT)

And have you entirely forgotten the encouraging words God spoke to you, his children? He said, "My child, don't ignore it when the Lord disciplines you, and don't be discouraged when he corrects you. For the Lord disciplines those he loves, and he punishes those he accepts as his children."

My Steps...

Father in the name of Jesus, I thank you for this time of prayer and for this moment to talk with you and you with me. Thank you Lord for your ministers of the gospel. It tells me that when things seem rough, I still have hope in the word of God. You tell me that if my life is full of difficulties and temptations, then be happy. When my way is rough then my patience has a chance to grow. You tell me to let it grow and don't try to squirm out of my problems. When my patience is finally in full bloom, then I will be ready for anything, strong in character, full and complete. Lord I thank you.

For when you punish me it proves you love me and I am your child. And as your child my gift is being able to speak in tongues, which is a language I have never learned, I will be speaking to God and not to others. You say that I will not be able to understand it for I will be speaking by the power of the Spirit and it will all be a secret to me. For when things seem rough, and I do not know what to say, the Holy Spirit will pray for me in tongues, making intercession in my spirit, for the Spirit is making intercession with moanings that cannot be uttered. Thank you for the gift of tongues and for allowing me to do spiritual warfare and spiritual combat in the spirit, with a language that I could not have studied, in Jesus name. Amen.

When You See It...
(Write Your Vision)

_____

_____

_____

_____

_____

Then You'll Say It...
(Speak the Vision)

_____

_____

_____

_____

_____

And You'll Have it!
(Write an Action Plan)

_____

_____

_____

_____

_____

Day 25
"God Keeps Me Safe and Secure"

We live in a world of uncertainty, which can breed a degree of anxiety about safety. This is not to be the case for children of God. He gives us the promise that He is constantly at watch over us and will protect us from anything that threatens to bring us harm.

His Steps...

Jude 1:21 (NLT)
Live in such a way that God's love can bless you as you wait for the eternal life that our Lord Jesus Christ in his mercy is going to give you.

1 Peter 1:5 (NLT)
And God, in his mighty power, will protect you until you receive this salvation, because you are trusting him. It will be revealed on the last day for all to see.

Psalm 23:6 (KJV)
Surely goodness and mercy shall follow me all the days of my life: and I will dwell in the house of the LORD for ever.

My Steps...

Father in the name of Jesus, I thank you for another day. I appreciate the opportunity to talk to you this day. You have been so good to me, to my family, my community and my church. Lord I just thank you for so much, so many blessings, so many things that I am enjoying because of what your son, Jesus, did at Calvary. I thank you for it. I come Lord to thank you for the safety and security you have provided me. Lord, so many people live in foreign lands, even here in our own nation we lack safety and people don't feel secure. We have those who are without hope, but I thank you that you have wrapped me in the blanket of security, and that security is your word. You have given me your precious word.

Lord, thank you that you have kept me from accidents. Thank you Lord you didn't have to do it but you did, and for this I want to say thank you. Thank you for your word that says, 'goodness and mercy shall follow me all the days of my life and I will dwell in the house of the Lord forever.' This is my prayer, in Jesus name, Amen.

When You See It...
(Write Your Vision)

_____
_____
_____
_____
_____

Then You'll Say It...
(Speak the Vision)

_____
_____
_____
_____
_____

And You'll Have it!
(Write an Action Plan)

_____
_____
_____
_____
_____

Day 26
"He Will Never Leave Me"

God has shown me that He will never leave me
by _____

_____

_____

_____

_____

His Steps...

Isaiah 41:17 (NLT)
"When the poor and needy search for water and
there is none, and their tongues are parched from
thirst, then I, the LORD, will answer them. I, the
God of Israel, will never forsake them.

Isaiah 55:2-3 (NLT)
Why spend your money on food that does not give
you strength? Why pay for food that does you no
good? Listen, and I will tell you where to get food
that is good for the soul!

"Come to me with your ears wide open. Listen, for
the life of your soul is at stake. I am ready to make
an everlasting covenant with you. I will give you all
the mercies and unfailing love that I promised to
David."

My Steps...

Father in the name of Jesus, thank you for your promises to me. You promised me that you would never leave me, nor would you forsake me, and you told me that it wasn't by might nor by my power, but it was by your spirit that I had not been consumed. Lord, I thank you that your spirit goes before me and it removes, pulls down, and puts up a defense for anything that would come after me or comes to hurt me. I am grateful that you protect me from it.

You also said that you would bring blind Israel along a path they had not seen before, you would make the darkness light before them, and smooth and straighten out the road ahead. I know these promises belong to me as well. I know you will not forsake me. I am confident in your promise to always be with me even until the end of the world. And for that I say thank you. Keep me near you always. Thank you, Jesus!

Now unto him that is able to keep you from falling, thank you Lord for keeping me faultless (sinless) before your power and grace, in your presence'. I thank you for it and appreciate you so much. Lord, and God, I ask that you have your way this day. This is my prayer in Jesus' name, Amen.

When You See It...
(Write Your Vision)

_____

_____

_____

_____

_____

Then You'll Say It...
(Speak the Vision)

_____

_____

_____

_____

_____

And You'll Have it!
(Write an Action Plan)

_____

_____

_____

_____

_____

Day 27
"I Have Mighty Weapons for War"

I will live like a Spirit-Controlled life by: _____

_____

_____

_____

His Steps...

2 Corinthians 10:4 (KJV)
(For the weapons of our warfare are not carnal, but mighty through God to the pulling down of strong holds;)

Ecclesiastes 9:18 (KJV)
Wisdom is better than weapons of war: but one sinner destroyeth much good.

Pslam 22:3 (KJV)
But thou art holy, O thou that inhabitest the praises of Israel.

Pslam 47:1-3 (KJV)
O clap your hands, all ye people; shout unto God with the voice of triumph. For the LORD most high is terrible; he is a great King over all the earth. He shall subdue the people under us, and the nations under our feet.

Isaiah 58:6 (KJV)
Is not this the fast that I have chosen? to loose the bands of wickedness, to undo the heavy burdens, and to let the oppressed go free, and that ye break every yoke?

Mark 9:29 (KJV)
And he said unto them, This kind can come forth by nothing, but by prayer and fasting.

My Steps...

Father in the name of Jesus, I thank you for your wonderful word, for it bring life to me daily. I thank you for desiring that I may know you more and for the fellowship we have over your word. Thank you for letting me know that you only want those things that are best for me.

Lord, thank you for the Holy Spirit that abides with me. Thank you that He is guiding me in every area of my life. Thank you that I obey His leading and can see the benefit of His control in my life. Thank you for every good and perfect gift that You have made known to me and I thank you for a greater walk of surrender to you, in Jesus' name. Amen.

When You See It...
(Write Your Vision)

_____
_____
_____
_____
_____

Then You'll Say It...
(Speak the Vision)

_____
_____
_____
_____
_____

And You'll Have it!
(Write an Action Plan)

_____
_____
_____
_____
_____

Day 28
"God Leads Me on My Path"

There is a path for every person born on this earth. But every person will not take the path laid out for them if they don't submit themselves to God, in order to find out what that path will yield for their lives.

His Steps...

Psalms 16:11 (KJV)

_____
_____
_____

Psalms 27:11 (KJV)

_____
_____
_____

Proverbs 5:6 (KJV)

_____
_____
_____

Joel 2:8 (KJV)

_____
_____
_____

My Steps...

Father in the name of Jesus, I thank you for Your word. For you said that I should meditate in it day and night, that I would make my own way prosperous, and I would have good success. This book of the law shall not depart out of my mouth. Thank you for helping me to keep your word before my eyes and in my heart.

O, God, help me in all that I do, that I would acknowledge you, so you will direct my path. I know if you direct my path I will always succeed. I know that success is in you and that you have ordained that I am always successful and on top and never at the bottom, because I will always seek you first. Thank you, Lord. In Jesus name, Amen.

When You See It...
(Write Your Vision)

_____

_____

_____

_____

_____

Then You'll Say It...
(Speak the Vision)

_____

_____

_____

_____

_____

And You'll Have it!
(Write an Action Plan)

_____

_____

_____

_____

_____

Day 29
"I Strive to Live a Fruitful Life"

As we go about our daily lives it is very easy to become overwhelmed with day-to-day obligations. Sometimes we can go for long periods of time without ever impacting someone else's life and bear very little fruit from our own. But the rewards are great when we can move on beyond this level of living into something more fulfilling and purposeful.

His Steps...

Psalm 3:8 (NLT)
Victory comes from you, O LORD. May your blessings rest on your people.

John 13:17 (KJV)

If ye know these things, happy are ye if ye do them.

I Peter 4:13 (NLT)
Instead, be very glad—because these trials will make you partners with Christ in his suffering, and afterward you will have the wonderful joy of sharing his glory when it is displayed to all the world.

Matthew 7:12 (KJV)
Therefore all things whatsoever ye would that men should do to you, do ye even so to them: for this is the law and the prophets.

My Steps...

Father in the name of Jesus, you told me that early in the morning before the sun comes up is the best time to pray. You promised to bless me with peace. I will pray morning, noon and night, pleading aloud with you and you will hear and answer me. Though the tide of the battle runs strongly against me, so many are fighting me, yet you will rescue me. Hallelujah!

You told me that you would keep me in perfect peace when my mind is focused on you. You told me that you would be with me. You said that a person who is speaking in tongues helps himself grow spiritually. One who prophesies or preaches messages from God helps the entire Church grow in holiness and happiness. God you let me know that if I pray in the spirit, my understanding would be fruitful, my spirit would be glorified, and my spirit would be lifted.

Thank you Lord for letting me know its right to pray according to your word, and if I pray according to your word, I have confidence that my prayers will be answered. Thank you for the word. Bless me now. Give victory, is my prayer in Jesus' name. Amen.

When You See It...
(Write Your Vision)

_____
_____
_____
_____
_____

Then You'll Say It...
(Speak the Vision)

_____
_____
_____
_____
_____

And You'll Have it!
(Write an Action Plan)

_____
_____
_____
_____
_____

Day 30
"I Know He is My Source"

There is power that comes from praying in the Holy Spirit. It is one of the weapons/gifts that God gives to believers. There is power in praying in the Spirit.

His Steps...

Acts 8:14-17 (NLT)
When the apostles back in Jerusalem heard that the people of Samaria had accepted God's message, they sent Peter and John there. As soon as they arrived, they prayed for these new Christians to receive the Holy Spirit. The Holy Spirit had not yet come upon any of them, for they had only been baptized in the name of the Lord Jesus. Then Peter and John laid their hands upon these believers, and they received the Holy Spirit.

Romans 1:19 (KJV)
Because that which may be known of God is manifest in them; for God hath shewed it unto them.

1 Corinthians 12:7 (KJV)
But the manifestation of the Spirit is given to every man to profit withal.

1 Corinthians 3:21(KJV)
Therefore let no man glory in men. For all things are your's;

Acts 17:28 (KJV)
For in him we live, and move, and have our being; as certain also of your own poets have said, For we are also his offspring.

John 14:16-17 (NLT)
And I will ask the Father, and he will give you another Counselor, who will never leave you. He is the Holy Spirit, who leads into all truth. The world at large cannot receive him, because it isn't looking for him and doesn't recognize him. But you do, because he lives with you now and later will be in you.

My Steps...
(Write your own prayer in the space provided)

Father in the name of Jesus, I thank you for

_____

_____

_____

_____

_____

_____

Lord, _____

_____

_____

_____

_____

_____

_____

in Jesus name, Amen.

When You See It...
(Write Your Vision)

_____
_____
_____
_____
_____

Then You'll Say It...
(Speak the Vision)

_____
_____
_____
_____
_____

And You'll Have it!
(Write an Action Plan)

_____
_____
_____
_____
_____

Contact the Author

Bishop George Copeland

P. O. Box 186
Salisbury, MD 21801-0186
Phone: 410-546-5577
E-Mail: bishopcopeland1@earthlink.net

Printed in the United States
35172LVS00001B/112-183

9 780976 369899